Down the Colorado

John Wesley Powell,
the One-Armed Explorer

Down the Colorado

John Wesley Powell, the One-Armed Explorer

Deborah Kogan Ray

Frances Foster Books
Farrar, Straus and Giroux
New York

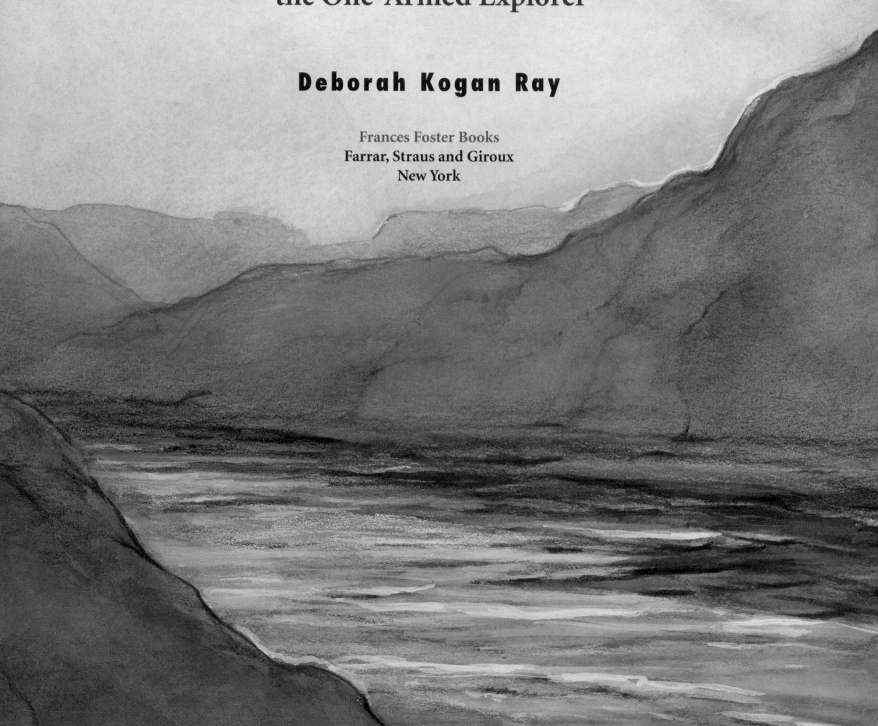

Jackson, Ohio, 1841

Everyone in the town of Jackson knew Wes Powell's father. Sunday mornings, he mounted the pulpit and delivered fiery sermons condemning slavery.

Feelings ran strong on both sides of the slavery question in southern Ohio. Most of the townspeople favored it, and their anger at crusading abolitionists, like the Reverend Joseph Powell, spilled over to their children. Seven-year-old Wes was often taunted because of his father. One day, he ran home from school, bloody and crying. His classmates had beaten and stoned him.

After that, Wes's mother, Mary Dean Powell, would not permit him to return to school, so a neighbor, George Crookham—a self-taught naturalist—offered to tutor him. Big George, as he was called, was an abolitionist whose farm was a stop on the Underground Railroad for runaway slaves.

A warm-hearted giant of a man, he had befriended the Powells when they first arrived from New York State, three years earlier, with their few possessions in a covered wagon. He had become a frequent guest in their busy household, where small, shy Wes would sit enrapt, listening to the huge old man describe the wonders of nature.

The Student

Big George believed that all things about nature should be learned by observation and experience. Wes followed him through tall grass fields and into thick forests in search of plants, insects, and reptiles. They waded into shallow ponds to study the construction of beaver dams. At Salt Lick Creek, they explored salt-crusted caverns where the walls tasted briny. Wes learned to identify the rocks along the banks by their mineral content and strata.

The nearby Scioto River was home to freshwater clams, snails, and mollusks that they collected to study in Big George's laboratory. The ancient arrowheads and pottery relics that they dug from mysterious earthen mounds beside the river fascinated the boy. He wondered about the native people who had lived there and made those things before written history.

After evening prayers, Wes read the natural history books that Big George lent him.

Wes's father valued education, but he did not approve of the study of natural science. To his mind, religion answered all questions about the world's order. As stern a man in his home as when delivering a sermon, he often reminded his son that he had been named John Wesley in honor of the man who founded their Methodist religion. The Reverend Powell never doubted that his son would become a minister.

But Wes had another calling.

He loved to explore the outdoors. He had a hunger to learn everything about it.

The Westward Move

Year by year, hostility toward the abolitionists escalated—their crop fields were destroyed, houses ransacked, suspected stops on the Underground Railroad burned. After an angry mob set George Crookham's laboratory ablaze, the Powells sold their small farm and prepared for a westward move to the Wisconsin frontier.

Sacks of seed grain, farm implements, tables, and beds were packed into the wagon. Wes comforted his mother when she had to abandon her beloved piano because it would not fit. He held back his tears when he said goodbye to Big George, and told himself he must behave like a man.

The Reverend Powell would be away from home for months at a time, traveling from community to community as a circuit preacher. Wes, at twelve years old, was now responsible for his family—his mother, two younger brothers, and five sisters.

Wes had no time for school when they moved to Wisconsin. His farm work began long before the sun came up and ended after dark. He stole reading time from the middle of the night when he should have been sleeping.

Time was scarce, but so were books. Wes hungrily awaited the packages of botany, zoology, and geology books that Big George sent, and then he waited for Sunday, when his family observed the Sabbath as a day of rest. Free from farm work at last, he escaped into the surrounding woods to read or follow winding creeks wherever they led him.

The Teacher

When the family moved to a new farm on the Illinois prairie, Reverend Powell insisted that Wes, now seventeen, prepare to enter the ministry.

But Wes refused. He was determined to pursue the path of science.

Although Wes had no formal education, he was well enough read to get a job teaching in a rural one-room schoolhouse. His plan was to earn money to enroll in college and to explore the Midwest in search of natural history specimens.

On a trip to Michigan, he met a cousin, Emma Dean. She was bright and beautiful and shared his love of science and adventure. From their first conversation at a family picnic, he knew he loved her. She encouraged him to follow his dreams.

It would not be an easy task. For ten years he taught school while taking courses in Greek and Latin, advanced mathematics, engineering, and all the natural sciences at colleges in Illinois and Ohio.

He made solitary rowboat expeditions to collect shells and minerals, traveling the length of the Ohio River, and descended down the Mississippi River from St. Paul, Minnesota, to New Orleans and the Gulf of Mexico.

In letters to Emma he described the sights and smells, the beauty and mystery of river travel: his anticipation of new discoveries to be made around every bend.

They corresponded constantly and made plans to marry.

The Soldier

On April 12, 1861, the Confederate forces—the army of the Southern states—fired on Fort Sumter, a Union garrison in South Carolina's Charleston harbor.

America's Civil War began.

Wes, like his father, was an avowed abolitionist. When President Abraham Lincoln issued a call for troops to defend the anti-slavery Union, he immediately enlisted in the army.

With the inevitability of battle fast approaching, Wes requested permission from his commanding officer, Major-General Ulysses S. Grant, for a short leave to go to Michigan to marry his beloved Emma.

On November 28, 1861, they were married at her father's house in Detroit. There was no honeymoon. Two hours after the ceremony, they were on a train bound for Cape Girardeau in Missouri, where Wes was training troops to fire cannons.

In the spring of 1862, his regiment—the 2nd Illinois Artillery Volunteers—was sent to Pittsburg Landing on the Tennessee River. Here, near a small meetinghouse called Shiloh Church, more than a hundred thousand men from the North and South fought in the war's first great bloody clash.

Twenty-three thousand soldiers would lose their lives, and many thousands more would be injured.

On the first day of the Battle of Shiloh, Captain John Wesley Powell raised his hand to signal for his gunners to fire. A minié ball struck his wrist, shattering his right arm.

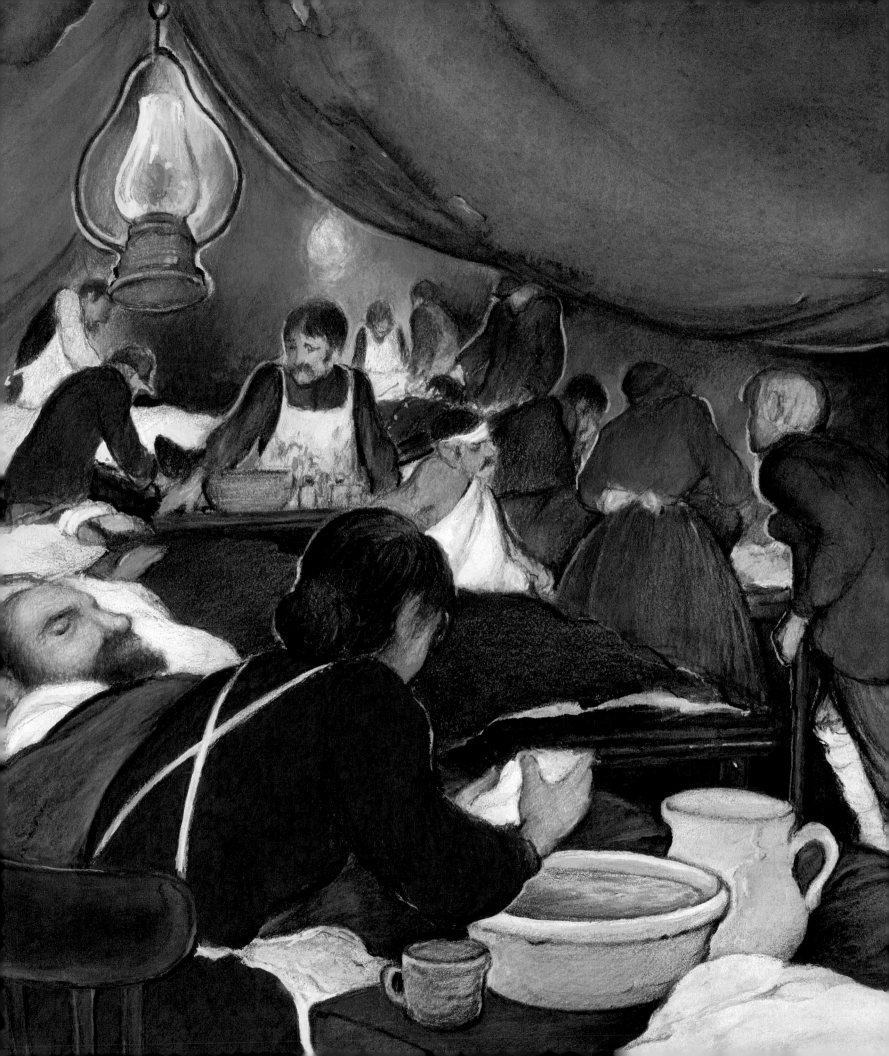

The Hospital

Two days later, his arm became infected and was amputated just below the elbow.

Medicine was very primitive in the Civil War—the only treatment for an infected arm or leg was to cut off the limb. There was often no anesthetic to be given, nothing to kill the pain during the operation or afterward. Doctors didn't yet understand the need to wash their hands or sterilize their surgical instruments to prevent infections.

Makeshift hospitals were set up in town halls, barns, and churches. They were crowded and dirty. There was a shortage of nurses to tend the injured. Emma arrived on the first available train to take care of her husband.

After his wound healed, Wes could have gone home because of his disability. Instead, he chose to remain in the army—determined to go on fighting for a righteous cause.

By the time he was discharged, three years later, he had fought in battles throughout the South, including the forty-day Siege of Vicksburg. He had been decorated for heroism, been promoted to the rank of major, and endured another operation on his arm. He weighed just 110 pounds, and his sleep was haunted by nightmares.

The Veteran

General Robert E. Lee surrendered his Confederate Army on April 9, 1865.

Less than a week later, John Wilkes Booth assassinated President Abraham Lincoln.

Wes and Emma waited outside the Chicago railroad station, with thousands of other mourners, for the funeral train carrying President Lincoln's body home to Springfield, Illinois.

Wes had gone to war for the beliefs he shared with Lincoln. Now he had come home to Illinois to say goodbye to his dead hero, and to try to pick up the pieces of his own life.

His father and many others viewed Wes as handicapped, and urged him to accept his limitations. His arm was always painful, but that was not what troubled him. The pain was in his heart. He had seen too much killing and too much suffering.

At Emma's urging, he took a position teaching geology at Illinois Wesleyan University in Bloomington, where he had studied before the war. But he felt imprisoned in the classroom.

Wes needed woods to roam in, rivers to follow, and the freedom of the outdoors. He began to teach as he had been taught by Big George Crookham—by direct experience with nature. Slowly, he began to mend.

The Rockies, 1867

Wes became determined that the loss of his arm would not keep him from new scientific explorations. In the summer of 1867, he and Emma led a group of students on a field trip to collect mineral specimens in Colorado.

The party traveled by train, wagon, and horseback across the plains to Denver and on to the Front Range, on the eastern side of the Rocky Mountains.

Wes and Emma climbed Pikes Peak. They explored dense forests and camped alongside rushing rivers. Alpine plants made a flowery carpet on the mountain slopes and ridges. It was the wildest, most wonderful country they had ever seen.

One night, their mountain guide, Jack Sumner, spoke of the unexplored canyon lands of the Colorado River—a vast unmapped area on America's face.

Wes listened to descriptions of roaring rapids and towering cataracts, to stories of adventurers who had attempted to run the river and never returned. Many native people believed that to enter the canyon was to disobey the gods. He was warned that the trip was impossible. But Wes didn't care. In his heart he knew he must go down the unknown river.

The White River

The following summer, Wes and Emma returned to the Rockies to lead another expedition. He had promised to collect natural history specimens for the university and several museums, and the Powells' plan was to remain in the Colorado Territory through the winter.

After most of the students returned to school, Wes and Emma and a few volunteers crossed the mountains to the western slope and set up camp along the White River. This was Ute country, roadless except for game and native trails.

Wes immediately befriended their Ute neighbors, and set about learning to speak their language. They called him Kapurats—"One-Arm-Off." With their guidance, he explored southward to the Grand River—as the upper Colorado was then called—northward to the Yampa, and around the Uinta Mountains.

His plan for exploration of the unknown canyon lands grew into a sweeping study involving mapping, natural history collecting, and a geologic survey of the entire area—an ambitious project, and one that would be very costly.

Plans for the Journey

Wes went to Washington, D.C., seeking financial support for a scientific expedition down the Colorado River, and was laughed at in government offices. An unknown one-armed geology professor conquering such a vast, dangerous, unexplored territory seemed preposterous.

Convinced that the journey was possible and that he could do it, he would not be deterred, and proceeded on his own. He scraped together a few donations, added all his personal savings, and made an agreement with the Illinois Museum of Natural History in Normal, Illinois, for use of scientific equipment in exchange for all the materials he would collect on the journey. Using his status as a decorated Civil War hero, he arranged for permission to obtain food at cost from military stores.

He designed four wooden expedition boats. Three were large and rugged, to carry heavy supplies, and constructed of sturdy oak. The fourth, a smaller pilot boat, was made of pine, to be light and maneuverable. The boats were built in Chicago and shipped west by rail.

Emma would stay behind in Detroit with her parents and report on the progress of the expedition to the newspapers as she received letters from Wes.

Green River City, Wyoming Territory, 1869

On May 24, 1869, John Wesley Powell and his crew of nine men set out from Green River City in Wyoming Territory. Their cargo was divided evenly between the three large boats, which each carried nearly a ton of supplies. There was enough flour, sugar, bacon, beans, dried apples, and coffee for the planned ten-month expedition. They had guns and traps for animal hunting and tools for boat repair and camping and for scientific work: two sextants, four chronometers, barometers, thermometers, and compasses.

Wes had recruited some of the crew members in town and knew others from his prior trips. Several were Civil War veterans, used to army discipline.

His crew on the small pilot boat, the *Emma Dean*, included Jack Sumner, his wilderness guide on the 1867 Rocky Mountain trip, who now acted as the expedition's second in command, and William Dunn, a hunter. Walter Powell, Wes's younger brother, and George Bradley—both officers during the Civil War—were on *Kitty Clyde's Sister*.

The crew of the ill-fated *No Name* was Oramel Howland, a printer and editor from Denver, his younger brother Seneca, and Frank Goodman, a British adventurer who had begged Wes to let him join the party. *Maid of the Canyon* carried Billy Hawkins, the expedition cook, and Andy Hall, who though only nineteen years old had already spent several years roaming the West, working as a mule driver and boatman.

The good people of Green River City turn out to see us start. We raise our little flag, push the boats from shore, and the swift current carries us down.

The "Emma Dean" goes in advance: the other boats follow, in obedience to signals.

A flag waved to the left or right meant to proceed in that direction; when waved down, it alerted the crews to land at once because of approaching danger.

The crews rowed in the traditional manner, facing upstream—blind to what was coming and stealing backward glances for directions. Each day brought a new set of challenges as they learned how to handle the heavy, laden boats, but the first eighty miles on the river passed without any serious problems. The upper Green, though swift, was shallow, and when it was interrupted by fast-running rapids, the men thrilled at the ride.

Beyond the towering Gates of Lodore—as they named the dark, narrow passage— they learned how dangerous the river could be. As they approached a fall, Wes signaled for the boats to stop. But the crew of the *No Name* missed his warning. The Howland brothers and Frank Goodman were thrown into the roiling river and caught by the current as Wes and the other crews struggled to rescue them. Fortunately, no one drowned. But the boat was shattered on the rocks, its cargo swept away.

Only sixteen days into their journey, and they had lost a boat and a third of their food supplies.

They named the spot Disaster Falls.

A ten-month expedition was now impossible.

Running rapids was the fastest way to put miles behind them, but after Disaster Falls, Wes became more cautious and ordered the men to portage the heavy boats and supplies around the worst rapids. This backbreaking work slowed their progress. Hundreds of pounds of supplies had to be unloaded at the top, the boats lowered by rope through the rapid, the supplies carried down and then reloaded below. The struggling crew slid on rocks, got bruised and battered, and grumbled.

Having experienced enough river danger, crew member Frank Goodman decided to remain at the Uinta Reservation Indian Agency Office when he and Wes hiked out forty miles to replenish supplies and mail letters.

Though Wes never allowed his missing arm to hamper his activities, it put him in danger on several occasions. He almost lost his life on a trip to measure the walls in Desolation Canyon. Clinging to a rock face with his one good arm, he was saved by George Bradley, who took off his pants and used them to pull Wes up to safety.

The Great Unknown

We are now ready to start on our way down the Great Unknown . . .
We have an unknown distance yet to run, an unknown river to explore. What
falls there are, we know not; what rocks beset the channel, we know not; what walls rise
over the river, we know not.

On the evening of July 16, the expedition reached the junction of the Green and the Grand rivers, where they camped for four days, exploring the surrounding area and repairing the boats and scientific equipment.

From here on, there were no known settlements, only the river to follow until the end of the unmapped canyons.

On the morning of July 21, they started down the Colorado.

The rapids were bigger, rougher, and closer together than ever. Most required long, hard portages—often several in a day. The river was a confusion of rocks and whirlpools; the boats banged into rocks, slammed against the raging water. Oars were lost, the boat bottoms cracked and splintered. Time was lost when the men had to stop to make repairs. And their food supply dwindled because of rot from constant soaking.

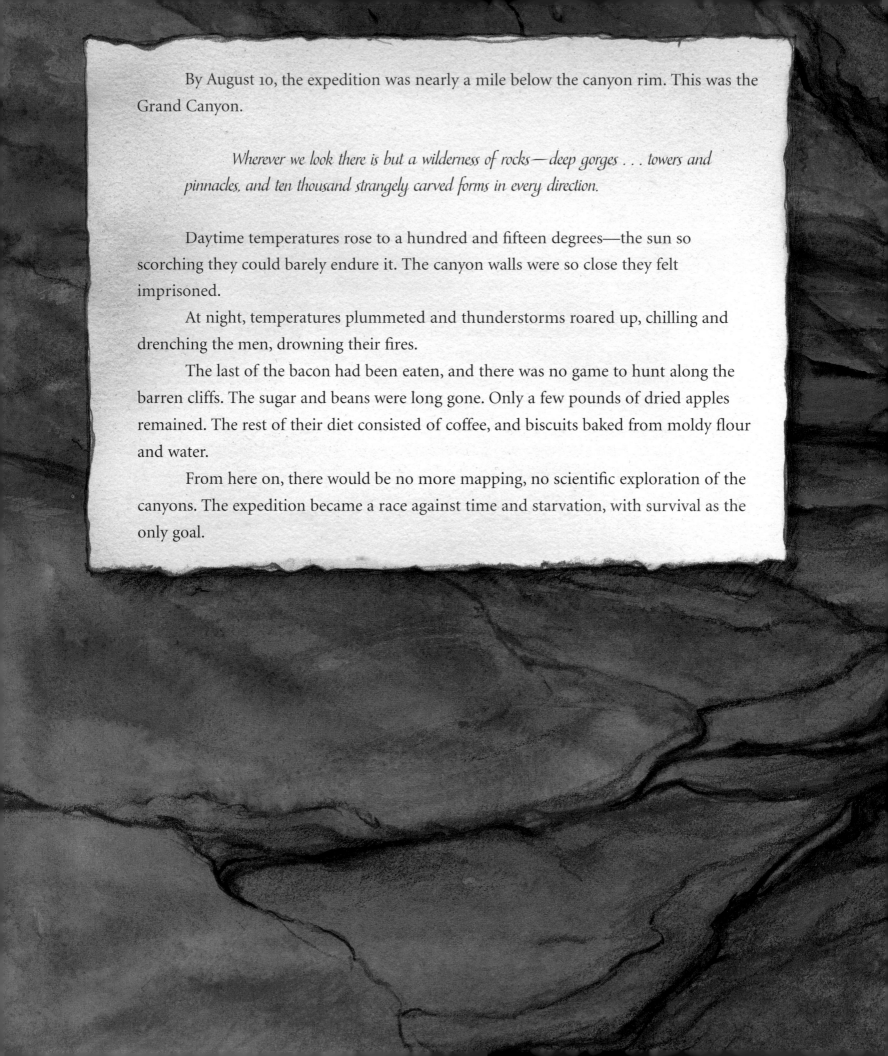

By August 10, the expedition was nearly a mile below the canyon rim. This was the Grand Canyon.

Wherever we look there is but a wilderness of rocks—deep gorges . . . towers and pinnacles, and ten thousand strangely carved forms in every direction.

Daytime temperatures rose to a hundred and fifteen degrees—the sun so scorching they could barely endure it. The canyon walls were so close they felt imprisoned.

At night, temperatures plummeted and thunderstorms roared up, chilling and drenching the men, drowning their fires.

The last of the bacon had been eaten, and there was no game to hunt along the barren cliffs. The sugar and beans were long gone. Only a few pounds of dried apples remained. The rest of their diet consisted of coffee, and biscuits baked from moldy flour and water.

From here on, there would be no more mapping, no scientific exploration of the canyons. The expedition became a race against time and starvation, with survival as the only goal.

At noon on the ninety-sixth day, Wes and his crew pulled to the side above a rapid, and stared in horror—the fall was more terrifying than any yet encountered. To the hungry, exhausted men, running the rapid looked like certain death. All afternoon, Wes climbed up and down the granite cliffs in search of a path around it, but there were barely any footholds. Portaging was impossible—they would have to run it. That night, three of the crew, the Howland brothers and William Dunn, told Wes that they would rather take their chances hiking out. He begged them to stay. There had been indications in the changing rock formations and elevations that they were nearing the end of the canyon. It might be only a day or two until they emerged—but he wasn't certain.

All night long I pace up and down a little path, on a few yards of sand beach, along by the river. Is it wise to go on? . . . To leave the exploration unfinished, to say that there is a part of the canyon which I cannot explore, having already nearly accomplished it, is more than I am willing to acknowledge, and I determine to go on.

At last daylight comes and we have breakfast without a word being said about the future . . . The last thing before leaving, I write a letter to my wife and give it to Howland . . . Some tears are shed . . . each party thinks the other is taking the dangerous course.

The three men began their long climb out of the canyon. The *Emma Dean* was left for them, in case they changed their minds. Then Wes and his remaining crew boarded the other two boats and pushed into the boiling rapid.

We are scarcely a minute in running it . . . We land at the first practicable point below, and fire our guns, as a signal to the men above that we have come over in safety. Here we remain a couple of hours, hoping that they will take the smaller boat and follow us . . . We wait until their coming seems hopeless, and then push on.

They named the spot Separation Rapid.

Wes would never see the men again. Later, he would learn that members of the Shivwits tribe, mistaking them for three marauders who had kidnapped and murdered a young woman from their village, had killed them.

Virgin River, Arizona Territory, 1869

On August 30, 1869, six men stepped ashore at the mouth of the placid Virgin River in the Arizona Territory. To their astonishment, three men and a boy greeted them by name. The men, residents of a nearby Mormon settlement, explained that they were expecting them—but dead. Newspaper stories reported the expedition had perished weeks ago. Brigham Young, the Mormons' leader in Salt Lake City, had sent orders to search the river for any bodies that had drifted downstream.

After ninety-nine days, one thousand miles, and five hundred rapids, Wes and his remaining crew of five had reached the end of their journey—the first recorded expedition to follow the Colorado River to the end of the Grand Canyon.

Mountains of music swell in the rivers, hills of music billow in the creeks, and meadows of music murmur in the rills that ripple over the rocks . . . The Grand Canyon is a land of song . . . Its walls and cliffs, its peaks and crags . . . tell a story of beauty and grandeur that I hear yet.

WYOMING
TERRITORY

MAY 24

MAY 30

JUNE 8

UINTA MOUNTAINS

GREEN RIVER

JUNE 25

JUNE 17

YAMPA RIVER

GREAT
SALT
LAKE

STATE OF NEVADA

UINTA RIVER

UINTA RESERVATION

WHITE RIVER

JUNE 28

COLORADO TERRITORY

JULY 8

UTAH
TERRITORY

DIRTY DEVIL RIVER

ESCALANTE RIVER

GRAND RIVER

JULY 16

JULY 23

JULY 29

VIRGIN RIVER

PARIA RIVER

SAN JUAN RIVER

AUGUST 5

KANAB CREEK

AUGUST 10

COLORADO RIVER

NEW MEXICO TERRITORY

AUGUST 25

AUGUST 15

LITTLE COLORADO RIVER

AUGUST 28

AUGUST 30

GRAND CANYON

ARIZONA TERRITORY

The Journey

Green River City

- MAY 24 Powell and his nine-man crew begin their journey.

Flaming Gorge

- MAY 30 The expedition encounters the first rapid-filled canyon.

Disaster Falls

- JUNE 8 One of the boats is destroyed; a third of their food supply, clothes, equipment, and scientific instruments is lost.

Echo Park

- JUNE 17 Wind spreads their campfire into the surrounding trees, and the fire grows quickly. They take to the boats and escape by running a rapid.

Split Mountain Canyon

- JUNE 25 The Green River carries them swiftly through the winding canyon.

Uinta River

- JUNE 28 They set up camp at the mouth of the river. Powell and three of the crew cross the desert to the Uinta Reservation—the last place to send mail and get supplies. Unknown to the expedition, on July 3, *The Chicago Tribune* headlines a story about their tragic end by drowning. It is based on a fabrication by a con man known as John Risdon, who claims to be the only survivor. The story creates a sensation and spreads across the wire services before Emma is able to refute it with a letter from Powell, sent from Green River City two weeks after the drowning supposedly occurred, that lists all the crew members—but not Risdon.

Desolation Canyon

- JULY 8 While measuring canyon walls, Powell is unable to climb up from a rocky ledge because of his missing arm. George Bradley takes off his pants and uses them to pull him to safety.

Junction of Green and Grand rivers

- JULY 16 They stop to repair the boats, to dry what food they can, and to map the area. On July 21, they start down the Colorado.

Cataract Canyon

- JULY 23 They encounter the worst rapids yet, which they battle through for several days.

Glen Canyon

- JULY 29 They enter a beautiful wooded canyon with sweeping rock formations that they name Glen Canyon.

Marble Canyon

- AUGUST 5 Past the mouth of the Paria River, they enter a canyon with sleek marble walls. They find moccasin prints along the riverbank—the first sign of other humans since leaving the Uinta Reservation.

The Grand Canyon

- AUGUST 10 Powell determines that the start of the Grand Canyon is the junction with the Little Colorado, and stops to take scientific measurements. Their food is fast diminishing and the crew become restless and angry.

Bright Angel Creek

- AUGUST 15 After days of portaging fierce rapids, they discover a tree-shaded creek. But they are soon back on the river and into even worse rapids. The heat is unbearable during the day, and it rains every night.

Lava Falls

- AUGUST 25 The rock formations change, which gives them hope that they may be nearing the end of the Grand Canyon.

Separation Rapid

- AUGUST 28 At what seems to them an impassable rapid, three of the crew choose to climb out of the canyon and hike cross-country. Powell and the remaining crew run the rapid.

Virgin River

- AUGUST 30 They float into the mouth of the Virgin River. The journey is over.

The map is based on the diaries and logs from Powell's 1869 expedition.

After the Journey

When news of the safe return of the expedition reached the outside world, John Wesley Powell became a national hero. He was invited to speak in cities throughout the country, where crowds flocked to hear his descriptions of the wondrous canyonlands of the Southwest. In Washington, D.C., Congress appropriated funds for the now famous Major Powell to explore the entire Colorado Plateau.

In 1871, he embarked on his second expedition down the Green and Colorado rivers. This time, with government backing, he brought photographers and artists who documented the amazing landscape. While a crew of geologists studied the physical history of the plateau, Powell immersed himself in the language and culture of the southwest desert's native peoples.

John Wesley Powell had great respect for Native Americans and defended their right to live according to their own traditions. His research of native cultures led to the creation of the Bureau of Ethnology at the Smithsonian Institution in Washington, D.C. He was appointed its first director in 1879 and held the position for the rest of his life.

In 1881, he became director of the U.S. Geological Survey, holding both positions simultaneously. Under his leadership, the agency established land and water surveys and topographic mapping throughout the country.

As a government official he fought, sometimes in vain, to protect and preserve the American West, urging care and reason in the use of its vast natural resources, and dignified treatment of its native peoples.

In 1903, a year after Powell died, President Theodore Roosevelt, an outdoorsman and advocate for preservation, first visited the Grand Canyon. He urged, "Do nothing to mar its grandeur, for the ages have been at work upon it . . . Keep it for your children, your children's children, and all who come after you."

John Wesley Powell would have agreed.

Author's Note

We are fortunate that firsthand accounts of the historic 1869 Colorado River expedition still exist. John Wesley Powell kept a daily journal, which he described as "long and narrow strips of brown paper, which were gathered into little volumes that were bound in sole leather in camp as they were completed." What remains of these slim volumes is archived in Washington, D.C., at the National Museum of Natural History. Crew member George Bradley kept a meticulous daily log, which now resides in the United States Library of Congress. And Jack Sumner and Billy Hawkins kept journals, which were later published as memoirs.

In 1875, the Smithsonian Institution published John Wesley Powell's *Exploration of the Colorado River of the West and Its Tributaries*, which covers his 1871 expedition as well.

I have used all these accounts to tell the story of the journey.

John Wesley Powell often returned to his beloved West to conduct scientific studies. In 1878, his report on the arid regions of the United States was published. It documented the terrain, water resources, and ecology and outlined a plan for responsible settlement.

As director of the U.S. Geological Survey, Powell believed it was his responsibility to protect the land and all who lived on it. This view brought him into sharp political conflict with those in the government who insisted on immediate westward expansion.

In 1888, Senator William Stewart of Nevada—a western land speculator with a vested interest in expansion—pushed a resolution through the U.S. Senate ordering Powell's agency to draw up immediate plans for dam construction to enable irrigation of the area for farming. When Powell refused, insisting that careful long-term planning was necessary to prevent soil erosion from severe droughts, Senator Stewart launched a vicious public smear campaign to remove him from his post. It was a battle that was to go on for six years, and one that Powell lost—the halls of government proving more difficult to conquer than the daunting canyons of the Colorado.

Heartbroken and in failing health, he wrote a letter of resignation to President Grover Cleveland on May 8, 1894, and retired from public life.

Sadly, Powell's prediction of severe droughts would come true.

The Colorado River that we see today, while still rapid-filled and fast-running, is not the wild river that Powell and his crew explored. Dams built for hydroelectric power and irrigation of the western states have tamed its waters in many places.

Separation Rapid no longer exists. In 1938, it was engulfed by the waters of Lake Mead, formed behind the giant Hoover Dam. The glorious two-hundred-mile Glen Canyon, explored and named by Powell and his crew, was dammed in 1963, creating a mammoth reservoir. Pleasure boats now cruise the calm waters—and it is named Lake Powell.

Chronology

John Wesley Powell (1834–1902)

1834   John Wesley Powell is born on March 24 in Mount Morris, New York.

1838   The family moves to Jackson in southern Ohio.

1846   The Powells move to Walworth County, Wisconsin.

1851   Wes begins teaching school in Jefferson County, Illinois.

1855   He meets his twenty-year-old cousin Emma Dean in Detroit.

1856–60   Studies at Illinois Wesleyan University, then at Oberlin College in Ohio. Collects fossils and freshwater shells on river expeditions.

1861   The Civil War begins on April 12. On May 6, Powell enlists as a private in the Union Army. On June 13, he is promoted to second lieutenant. On November 28, he marries Emma Dean.

1862   He is promoted to captain. On April 6, during the Battle of Shiloh, his right arm is shattered and then amputated below the elbow. He decides to remain in active service if Emma is granted a "perpetual pass" to accompany him wherever he is sent.

1863   He takes part in the Siege of Vicksburg (May 26–July 4) and is decorated for bravery. While convalescing from a second surgery on his arm, he is notified of his promotion to the rank of major.

1865   On January 4, he requests a discharge from the Union Army. The Civil War ends on April 9. Illinois Wesleyan University in Bloomington hires Powell as a professor of geology for the fall semester.

1867   On June 1, sets off on his first expedition to Colorado with Emma and ten students. Emma becomes the first woman known to have climbed Pikes Peak.

1868   He and Emma spend the winter in Colorado with the White River Ute tribe, camped in an area now called Powell Bottoms.

1869   May 24–August 30: Leads his first expedition down the Green and Colorado rivers. Becomes a national hero. Goes on the lecture circuit, visiting Denver, Chicago, and New York.

1871   Sets off on a second expedition down the Green and Colorado rivers on May 22. Emma has accompanied him as far as Salt Lake City, where their only child, Mary Dean Powell, is born on September 8.

1872–78   Moves to Washington, D.C. On trips to the southwest desert he establishes close ties with native tribes. He makes topographic and irrigation studies, and writes a report for the U.S. Secretary of the Interior.

1879   Smithsonian Institution sets up the Bureau of Ethnology (merged into the Department of Anthropology), which he directs for twenty-three years.

1881   He is appointed director of the U.S. Geological Survey.

1888   The U.S. Geological Survey is ordered to make immediate site plans for western dams. Powell insists on long-term planning, clashing with Senator Stewart of Nevada, who launches a campaign to remove him from office.

1894   On May 8, Powell resigns as director of the U.S. Geological Survey. Keeping his position at the Smithsonian, he devotes himself to ethnographic writing.

1902   On September 23, with Emma and his daughter at his side, John Wesley Powell dies at his home in Haven, Maine, at the age of sixty-eight. He is buried at Arlington National Cemetery, with the honors due a Civil War veteran. As he requested, Emma is buried beside him when she dies in 1924.

Bibliography

Cooley, John, ed. *Exploring the Colorado River: Firsthand Accounts by Powell and His Crew*. Mineola, N.Y.: Dover Publications, 2004.

Dolnick, Edward. *Down the Great Unknown: John Wesley Powell's 1869 Journey of Discovery and Tragedy Through the Grand Canyon*. New York: HarperCollins, 2001.

Lossing, Benson J. *Mathew Brady's Illustrated History of the Civil War*. New York: Portland House, n.d. Reprint; orig. pub. New York: War Memorial Association, 1912.

Pettit, Jan. *Utes: The Mountain People*. Rev. ed. Boulder, Colo.: Johnson Printing Company, 1990.

Porter, Eliot. *The Place No One Knew: Glen Canyon on the Colorado*. Edited by David Brower. San Francisco: Sierra Club, 1963.

Powell, John Wesley. "Down the Colorado: Diary of the First Trip Through the Grand Canyon 1869." First pub. in *Scribner's Monthly* in 1874–75 and in book form as *The Exploration of the Colorado River of the West and Its Tributaries*. Washington, D.C.: U.S. Government Printing Office, 1875. Repr. New York: Promontory Press, n.d.

———. *The Exploration of the Colorado River and Its Canyons*. New York: Dover Publications, 1961. Prev. pub. as *The Canyons of the Colorado*. New York: Flood and Vincent, 1895.

Stegner, Wallace. *Beyond the Hundredth Meridian: John Wesley Powell and the Second Opening of the West*. New York: Penguin Books, 1992.

Worster, Donald. *A River Running West: The Life of John Wesley Powell*. New York: Oxford University Press, 2001.

For Nicole

Distributed in Canada by Douglas & McIntyre Ltd.
Color separations by Chroma Graphics PTE Ltd.
Printed and bound in China by South China Printing Co. Ltd.
Designed by Barbara Grzeslo
First edition, 2007
1 3 5 7 9 10 8 6 4 2

www.fsgkidsbooks.com

Library of Congress Cataloging-in-Publication Data
Ray, Deborah Kogan, date.
   Down the Colorado : John Wesley Powell, the one-armed
explorer / Deborah Kogan Ray.— 1st ed.
       p.   cm.
   ISBN-13: 978-0-374-31838-3
   ISBN-10: 0-374-31838-7
   1. Powell, John Wesley, 1834–1902—Juvenile literature.
2. Explorers—West (U.S.)—Biography—Juvenile literature.
3. Colorado River (Colo.-Mexico)— Discovery and exploration—
Juvenile literature.   4. West (U.S.)—Discovery and exploration—
Juvenile literature.   I. Title.

F788.P88 R395 2007
917.91/3044092 B—dc22

                                        2006043994

Illustrations executed in transparent watercolor, gouache, and
colored pencil on Arches 140 lb. hot-press watercolor paper